Sustaining the (
When Images T

Sosteniendo la mirada:
cuando las imágenes tiemblan

Soutenant le regard:
quand les images tremblent

Sustaining the Gaze: When Images Tremble / Sosteniendo la mirada: cuando las imágenes tiemblan / Soutenant le regard: quand les images tremblent

Acknowledgements
This book's photographs and poems in Spanish and English were exhibited under the title *Sustaining the Gaze: When Images Tremble / Sosteniendo la mirada: cuando las imágenes tiemblan* in the Green Room, James Dunn Building, St Thomas University, Fredericton, March 2003. The poems in Spanish and English are reprinted from the book *During Nights that Undress Other Nights / En las noches que desvisten otras noches* (Fredericton NB: Broken Jaw Press, 2003) by Nela Rio, translations by Elizabeth Gamble Miller. Several of the poem translations into French by Jill Valéry have previously been published in the Nela Rio artist book *La voz del silencio / The Voice of Silence / La voix du silence* (Fredericton NB: Publicaciones La Candela, 1995).

Fotografía de / Photo of Nela Rio by Federico Hidalgo.
Fotografía de / Photo of Brian Atkinson by Glen D. Ross © 2003.
Design and in-house editing by the publisher, Joe Blades.
Printed and bound in Canada by Sentinel Printing, Yarmouth NS, Canada.

The publisher acknowledges the support of the Canada Council for the Arts and the New Brunswick Culture and Sport Secretariat — Arts Development Branch.

Broken Jaw Press Inc.
Box 596 Stn A
Fredericton NB E3B 5A6
Canada

www.brokenjaw.com
jblades@brokenjaw.com
tel/fax 506 454-5127

National Library of Canada Cataloguing in Publication Data

Atkinson, Brian, 1951-

Sustaining the gaze : when images tremble = Sosteniendo la mirada : cuando las imágenes tiemblan = Soutenant le regard : quand les images tremblent / photographs by Brian Atkinson ; poems by Nela Rio ; translation into English by Elizabeth Gamble Miller ; translation into French by Jill Valéry ; introduction by Joe Blades.

Text in English, Spanish and French.
Includes bibliographical references.
ISBN 1-55391-028-1

1. Atkinson, Brian, 1951- 2. Women—Guatemala—Pictorial works. 3. Women—Guatemala—Poetry. I. Rio, Nela II. Miller, Elizabeth Gamble, 1926- III. Valéry, Jill, 1941- IV. Title. V. Title: Sosteniendo la mirada. VI. Title: Soutenant le regard.

NX513.Z9A842 2004 779'.24"097281 C2004-900669-XE

Catalogage avant publication de la Bibliothèque nationale du Canada

Atkinson, Brian, 1951-

Sustaining the gaze : when images tremble = Sosteniendo la mirada : cuando las imágenes tiemblan = Soutenant le regard : quand les images tremblent / photographs by Brian Atkinson ; poems by Nela Rio ; translation into English by Elizabeth Gamble Miller ; translation into French by Jill Valéry ; introduction by Joe Blades.

Texte en anglais, en espagnol et en français.
Comprend des références bibliographiques.
ISBN 1-55391-028-1

1. Atkinson, Brian, 1951-. 2. Femmes—Guatemala—Ouvrages illustrés. 3. Femmes—Guatemala—Poésie. I. Rio, Nela II. Miller, Elizabeth Gamble, 1926- III. Valéry, Jill, 1941- IV. Titre. V. Titre: Sosteniendo la mirada. VI. Titre: Soutenant le regard.

NX513.Z9A842 2004 779'.24"097281 C2004-900669-XF

Sustaining the Gaze: When Images Tremble

Sosteniendo la mirada: cuando las imágenes tiemblan

Soutenant le regard: quand les images tremblent

photographs by Brian Atkinson

poems by Nela Rio

translation into English by Elizabeth Gamble Miller

translation into French by Jill Valéry

Introduction by Joe Blades

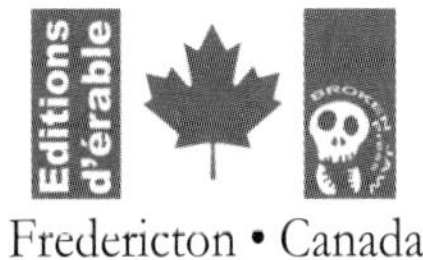

Fredericton • Canada

contents

Introduction

Last year …
last March, during Hispanic Week at St Thomas University, Nela Rio, Elizabeth Gamble Miller and I started talking about the possibility of publishing *During Nights that Undress Other Nights / En las noches que desvisten otras noches*, Nela Rio's third fully bilingual Spanish to English book with Broken Jaw Press.

Last year …
Nela Rio started talking with me about her ideas and plans for this year's International Week at St Thomas University, about partnering with the *FacingFaces* project. In an e-mail she sent me a link to the website for that project by Belgian artist Gino d'Artali living in Ciudad Juárez, México.

Last year …
Brian Atkinson loaned me a CD and a binder of his black and white photographs from Central and South America but taken primarily in southern México and Guatemala. For every photograph he had a story, sometimes two stories.

Last year …
during one of our many necessary multi-project update meetings, I showed Brian Atkinson's album of photographs to Nela Rio. She was immediately taken by them, by how the women in the photographs mirrored some of the women in her poetry, in her experience.

Last year …
Brian Atkinson decided that he wanted to travel to Guatemala, to revisit people and places where he'd last been six years before.

Last year …
Nela sent out the initial call to artists and poets inviting them to participate in *Outspoken Art / Arte Claro.*

Last year …
Brian e-mailed me while I was in Nova Scotia, wrote that I should find a copy of the January 2003 *PhotoLife* magazine. The cover photo, by Brian, is paired with the phrase "Sense of Purpose". Inside, the Gallery section of his photographs and the Profile essay by Peter K. Burian are both titled "A Commitment to Photojournalism in the Third World". At one point, the article quotes from a website: "Brian's photography is about people, the chance to live, learn and work with people all over the world, and to help them voice their story."

Last year …
I was finally able to arrange a meeting for early this year that the three of us were able to attend.

~ ~ ~

That meeting resulted in the photo essay *Sustaining the Gaze: When Images Tremble / Sosteniendo la mirada: cuando las imágenes tiemblan*, photos by Brian Atkinson, poems by Nela Rio, exhibited at St Thomas Universty with translations by Elizabeth Gamble Miller into English. This book is a second-stage result that also includes translations of Nela Rio's poems by Jill Valéry into French.

Brian Atkinson's photgraphs in this book were taken in Guatemala's Ixcan jungle between 1994 and 1997. These poems were inspired by Nela's translation of 1983 testimonials given by Guatemalan refugees.

~ ~ ~

Look at the photographs.
See the women in the photographs,
their journalistic portraits.
Imagine their lives.
Some live in battered villages and refugee camps.
Some live in a jungle with a gun in their hands,
on a break from defending themselves,
their families and way of life.
These women are not able to attend a gallery exhibition opening,
are not able to attend classes at university,
are not living in their homes,
are not going to market,
cannot sit in a café
a theatre,
a church,
even if they want to.

Read the poems.
These poems give voice to women,
women who have lived lives as best they can:
whether they've resisted the aggression,
raised their voices, their fists, their guns;
or tried to attend university to learn and better themselves;
or made homes and raised families.
These poems are dedicated to women who have suffered,
or who are still suffering,
grieving the loss of family members,
or they, themselves, are missing,
disappeared in the oubliettes

of torture and clandestine prisons.
These poems are their stories, their testimonials,
if only they could speak,
if they still live.
As Nela Rio says,
"These are poems for peace."

— Joe Blades
March 2003

Introducción

El año pasado ...
en marzo, durante la Semana Hispánica en St.Thomas University, Nela Rio, Elizabeth Gamble Miller y yo, comenzamos a hablar sobre la publicación de *En las noches que desvisten otras noches,* el tercer libro bilingüe de Nela Rio, del español al inglés, publicado por Broken Jaw Press.

El año pasado ...
Nela Rio comenzó a contarme sus ideas y planes para la Semana Internacional de 2003 en St. Thomas University, de cómo quería asociarla con el proyecto *FacingFaces.* Me mandó la dirección del portal en la Web dedicado al proyecto del artista belga Gino d'Artali, que vive en Ciudad Juárez, México.

El año pasado ...
Brian Atkinson me prestó un disco compacto y una carpeta de sus fotografías en blanco y negro de la América Central y de la América del Sur, tomadas principalmente en la parte sur de México y de Guatemala. Para cada una de las fotos tenía una historia, a veces dos.

El año pasado ...
durante una de esas necesarias reuniones en las que nos actualizamos mutuamente de nuestros múltiples proyectos, le mostré a Nela Rio el album de fotografías de Brian Atkinson. Quedó inmediatamente impresionada por la manera en que algunas de las mujeres de las fotos reflejaban a las mujeres en su propia poesía, en su propia experiencia.

El año pasado ...
Brian decidió que quería viajar a Guatemala, para volver a visitar a la gente y lugares donde había estado hacía ya seis años.

El año pasado…
Nela mandó el primer anuncio invitando a artistas y poetas a participar en *Outspoken Art / Arte Claro.*

El año pasado …
estaba yo en Nueva Escocia cuando Brian me mandó un mensaje electrónico diciéndome que debería buscar una copia de la edición de enero de 2003 de la revista *PhotoLife*. La foto en la tapa era de Brian y estaba unida a la frase "Con un sentido de propósito". En la sección *Galería*, las fotos de Brian y el ensayo de Peter K. Burian aparecen bajo el título "Un compromiso de Foto-periodismo con el Tercer Mundo". En el artículo hay una cita tomada de un portal de internet: "Las fotografías de Brian se centran en la gente: en la posibilidad de vivir, aprender y trabajar con gente de todo el mundo, y ayudarles a dar voz a su historia".

El año pasado …
Finalmente pude organizar una reunión para los comienzos de 2003 en la que nos encontraríamos los tres por primera vez.

~ ~ ~

El resultado de esa reunión fue el Foto-ensayo *Sustaining the Gaze: When Images Tremble / Sosteniendo la mirada: cuando las imágenes tiemblan*, fotos de Brian Atkinson, poemas de Nela Rio, que se exhibió en St. Thomas University con traducción al inglés de Elizabeth Gamble Miller. El presente libro, con la inclusión de la traducción al francés por Jill Valéry de los poemas de Nela Rio, representa una segunda etapa en la evolución del proyecto.

~ ~ ~

Miren las fotografías.
Vean a las mujeres en estas fotografías, su retrato periodístico.
Imaginen sus vidas.
Algunas viven en pueblos destruídos y en campos de refugiados.
Otras viven en la selva con armas en las manos,
en un descanso por la lucha por su propia defensa,
por la de sus familias y por su modo de vivir.
Estas mujeres no pueden asistir a la inauguración de una galería de
exposición como ésta,
ni pueden asistir a la universidad,
ni vivir en su casa,
ni ir al mercado,
ni pueden sentarse en un café
en un teatro
en una iglesia,
aunque quisieran.

Lean los poemas.
Estos poemas dan voz a las mujeres.
Mujeres que han vivido su vida como han podido:
sea resistiendo la agresión,
levantando sus voces, sus puños, sus armas;
o tratando de ir a la universidad para aprender y superarse;
o hacer sus hogares y mantener la familia.
Estos poemas están dedicados a mujercs que han sufrido,
o todavía sufren,
llorando por la pérdida de sus familiares,
o desaparecidas ellas mismas,
desaparecidos en las cámaras
de tortura y las prisiones clandestinas.
Estos poemas son sus historias, sus testimonios,

si sólo pudieran hablar,
si todavía estuvieran vivas.
Como Nela Rio dice
"Estos poemas son por la paz".

— Joe Blades
marzo 2003

Introduction

L'année passée ...
en mars, au cours de la Semaine hispanique à l'Université Saint-Thomas, Nela Rio, Elizabeth Gamble Miller et moi-même avons abordé une discussion de la publication éventuelle de *En las noches que desvisten otras noches / During Nights that Undress Other Nights,* le troisième des livres bilingues (espagnol / anglais) de Nela Rio parus chez Broken Jaw Press.

L'année passée ...
Nela Rio a commencé à me parler de ses idées et de ses projets pour la Semaine internationale à l'Université Saint-Thomas en 2003; elle m'a parlé également de son désir de participer au projet *FacingFaces*. Elle m'a envoyé par courriel le nom d'un lien au site Web consacré à ce projet, ce dernier créé par l'artiste belge Gino d'Artali, qui vit à Ciudad Juarez au Mexique.

L'année passée ...
Brian Atkinson m'a prêté une disquette et un classeur de ses photos en noir et blanc prises en Amérique Centrale, en Amérique du Sud et en particulier, au sud du Mexique et au Guatemala. Brian a raconté une histoire, parfois deux, pour chacune des photos.

L'année passée ...
au cours de l'une de nos nombreuses réunions, nécessaires pour nous tenir au courant de nos projets multiples, j'ai montré l'album de photos de Brian Atkinson à Nela Rio. Elle a tout de suite été impressionnée par la ressemblance qu'elle trouvait entre les femmes photographiées et certaines des femmes qui figurent dans ses poèmes.

L'année passée …
Brian Atkinson a décidé de voyager au Guatemala pour revoir les gens et les lieux qu'il avait connus six ans auparavant.

L'année passée …
Nela Rio a envoyé sa première invitation à des artistes et des poètes à participer au projet *Outspoken Art / Arte Claro.*

L'année passée …
j'étais en Nouvelle Écosse quand Brian Atkinson m'a envoyé un message par courriel: je devrais me procurer le numéro de janvier 2003 de la revue *PhotoLife* . Brian avait pris la photo de la page couverture qui allait de pair avec les mots; "La Résolution". La partie "Galérie" des photos de Brian, ainsi que l'essai-profil de Peter K. Burian, s'intitulait "Un engagement pour le photojournalisme dans le tiers monde". À un moment donné, l'article cite une phrase tirée d'un site Web : "Centrée sur les gens, la photographie offre à Brian l'occasion de vivre, d'apprendre et de travailler chez les gens aux quatre coins du monde, tout en les aidant à exprimer leur histoire".

L'année passée …
j'ai pu enfin organiser une réunion pour le début de l'an 2003 à laquelle nous avons pu assister tous les trois.

~ ~ ~

De cette réunion est né l'essai photographique *Sustaining the Gaze: When Images Tremble / Sosteniendo la mirada: cuando las imágenes tiemblan.* Les photos de Brian Atkinson et les poèmes de Nela Rio, avec leur traduction en anglais d'Elizabeth Gamble Miller, étaient le sujet d'une exposition à l'Université Saint-Thomas. Le livre actuel représente une deuxième étape dans l'évolution du projet par l'ajout de la traduction en français par Jill Valéry des poèmes de Nela Rio.

~ ~ ~

Regardez ces photos.
Voyez les femmes dans ces photos,
leur portrait journalistique.
Imaginez leur vie.
Les unes vivent dans des villages délabrés et dans des camps de réfugiés.
Les autres vivent dans la jungle, mitrailleuse à la main,
en un moment de repos dans leur défense
d'elles-mêmes,
de leur famille,
et de leur mode de vie.
Il est interdit à ces femmes d'assister à un vernissage,
et aux cours universitaires,
de demeurer dans leur demeure,
d'aller au marché,
de s'asseoir dans un cafe,
un théâtre, une église,
même si elles le désirent.

Lisez ces poèmes.
Ces poèmes donnent la parole aux femmes,
à des femmes qui ont vécu la vie en faisant de leur mieux:
qu'elles aient résisté à l'agression,
qu'elles aient menacé de la voix, du poing, du fusil;
ou qu'elles aient tenté de fréquenter l'université afin d'apprendre et de se cultiver; ou qu'elles aient créé des foyers pour y élever leur famille.
Ces poèmes sont dédiés à des femmes qui ont souffert,

ou qui souffrent toujours,
pleurant la perte de membres de leur famille,
ou qui sont elles-mêmes absentes,
disparues dans les oubliettes
de la torture et des prisons clandestines.
Ces poèmes sont leurs histoires, leurs témoignages,
si seulement elles pouvaient parler,
si elles vivent toujours.
Comme le dit Nela Rio :
"Ces poèmes sont pour la paix".

— Joe Blades
mars 2003

Sustaining the Gaze: When Images Tremble

Sosteniendo la mirada: cuando las imágenes tiemblan

Soutenant le regard: quand les images tremblent

Testimonies (excerpts)

(from Guatemalan refugees to the Comité Cristiano de Solidaridad, 1983, and to researchers in Canada. Names will not be disclosed.)

"I saw the soldiers burning the houses. My house is outside the village and I saw from there that they were burning the houses […]."

"In […] they killed the women by throwing bombs on them and later they killed the men. This way they killed everyone."

"[…] At 2:30 p.m. of the 19th of July I saw the smoke coming from the village of […]. The soldiers were burning the village […] I heard the screams of captured people.

"I continued on the road and before getting into […] I saw 12 bodies on the road, among them there were babies of 8 months, more or less. A lot of them had their heads split open. I saw that they had tortillas as if they were prepared for a trip. Everything was scattered around. […] One woman had been disemboweled and all her intestines were lying on the ground. Their heads were in pieces, their teeth broken. The majority were women. […] The women didn't have any clothes on, only something thrown over them. The soldiers had raped them. The soldiers covered the bodies with branches, as if to hide them. […] One of the peasants, waking along that road, came to the pile of bodies and recognized his family."

— translation from Spanish to English by Nela Rio

Testimonios (fragmentos)

(de refugiados guatemaltecos al Comité Cristiano de Solidaridad 1983, y a investigadores de Canadá. Los nombres no se harán públicos.)

"Mi casa está afuera de la aldea, lo miré que (los soldados) estaban quemando las casas [...]."

"En [...] mataron a las mujeres echándoles bombas [...] y luego a los hombres. Así fallecieron toda la gente."

"A las 2.30 de la tarde del día 19 de julio vi el humo de la aldea [...]. Los soldados estaban quemando las casas [...] oí los gritos de los capturados [...]."

"Seguí mi camino y antes de llegar a [...] vi 12 muertos en el camino, dentro de ellos hay dos niños como de ocho meses. Muchos de ellos partidos de la cabeza. Los muertos, se ve que llevaban tortillas como que fueran de viaje. Todas sus cosas estaban regadas. [...] A una mujer le quitaron las tripas que estaban regadas por el camino. Las cabezas estaban por pedazos, los dientes quebrados. La mayoría son mujeres [...]. Las mujeres estaban sin ropa, sólo les echaron los huipiles encima. Los soldados las habían violado. Les echaron monte encima, como para disimular los muertos." [...] Uno de los campesinos cuando caminaba por el mismo camino [...] se topó con el montón de muertos y pudo reconocer a su familia."

Témoignages (extraits)

(donnés par des réfugiés guatémaltèques au *Comité Cristiano de Solidaridad* en 1983 et à des recherchistes au Canada. Ni les noms des réfugiés ni ceux de leurs villages ne seront dévoilés.)

"J'ai vu les soldats mettre le feu aux maisons. Ma maison est située en dehors du village et de là j'ai vu qu'ils mettaient le feu aux maisons[…]"

"A […], ils ont tué les femmes en les bombardant et plus tard ils ont tué les hommes. De cette façon ils ont tué tout le monde."

[…] "A 14h, 30 du 19 juillet, j'ai vu de la fumée venant du village de […] Les soldats mettaient le feu au village […]. J'ai entendu les cris des gens capturés […]."

"J'ai continué mon chemin et avant d'arriver à […] j'ai vu 12 corps sur le chemin; parmi eux, il y avait des bébés de 8 mois, plus ou moins. Beaucoup d'entre eux avaient la tête fendue. J'ai vu qu'ils avaient apporté des *tortillas* comme s'ils étaient prêts pour un voyage. Tout était éparpillé aux alentours. […] On avait éviscéré l'une des femmes et tous ses intestins étaient par terre. Ils avaient la tête en morceaux, les dents cassées. La majorité était des femmes. […] Les femmes ne portaient pas de vêtements, seulement quelque chose qu'on avait jeté sur elles par la suite. Les soldats les avaient violées. Les soldats avaient couvert les corps avec des branches, comme pour les cacher. […] Un des paysans, lorsqu' il se promenait sur ce chemin-là, est arrivé aux corps entassés et il a reconnu sa famille. […]"

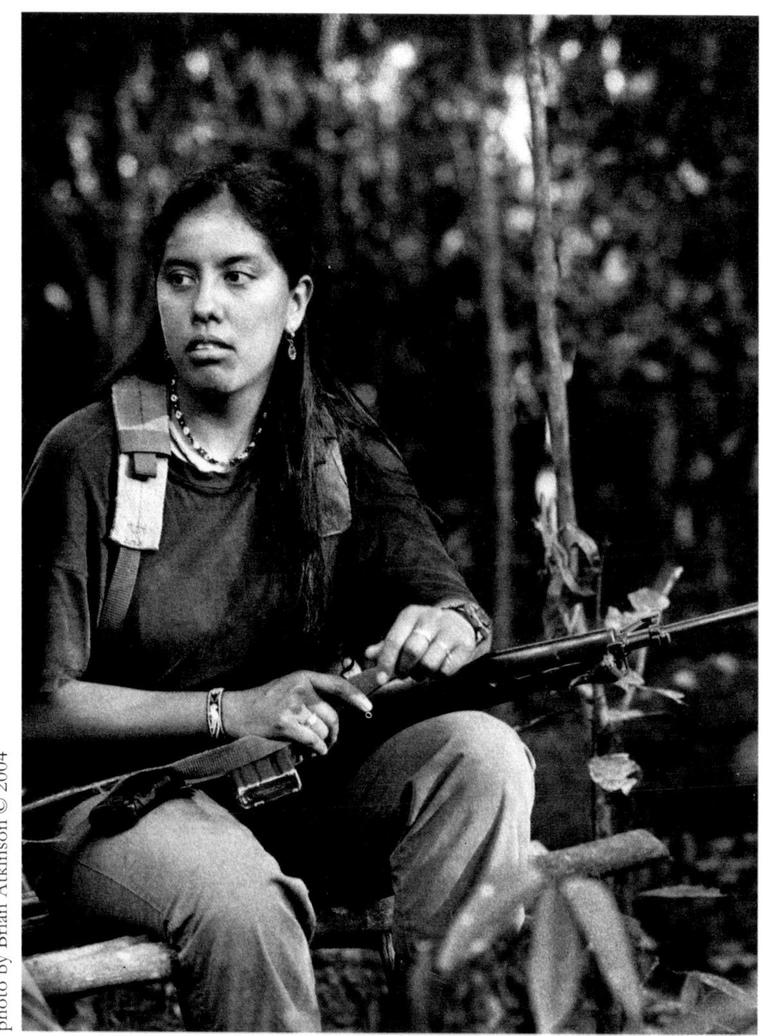

photo by Brian Atkinson © 2004

V

To Isabel, with respect

It is one in the afternoon
of any day
of a day that makes history
of the kind never told.

Today's sun stings hard
with the force of bullets
and no tree will offer shade
will shelter me
will cover me
will not kill

and the soldiers are closing in
like a cloud full of blood
striking, splattering
and I shrink
into my skin, into my shoes

and when I look at my hands
I see them full of blood
and when I look at my legs
I see them full of blood

and I sink my teeth into my heart
so they won't take it from me
and the blood that covers me
is the blood of my screams

and they carry away my blood
the soldiers
who carry a cloud full of the dead.

V

A Isabel, con respeto

Es la una de la tarde
de un día cualquiera
de un día que hace historia
de esa que nunca cuentan.

El sol pica hoy con la fuerza
de las balas
y no hay árbol que dé sombra
que me cubra
que me tape
que no mate

y los soldados se acercan
como una nube llena de sangre
sacudiendo, salpicando
y yo me encojo
en mi piel, en mis zapatos

y cuando miro mis manos
las veo llenas de sangre
y cuando miro mis piernas
las veo llenas de sangre

y aferro mi corazón con los dientes
para que no me lo quiten
y la sangre que me cubre
es la sangre de mis gritos

y a mi sangre se la llevan
los soldados
que cargan una nube llena de muertos.

V

Pour Isabel, avec respect

Il est une heure de l'après-midi
d'un jour quelconque
d'un jour qui fait date
celle que jamais on ne raconte.

Le soleil tape aujourd'hui avec la force
des balles
et il n'y a aucun arbre pour m'ombrager
pour me couvrir
pour me cacher
qui ne tue pas

et les soldats s'approchent
comme un nuage rempli de sang
me battant, m'éclaboussant
et moi je me resserre
dans ma peau, dans mes souliers

et quand je regarde mes mains
je les vois pleines de sang
et quand je regarde mes jambes
je les vois pleines de sang

et je saisis mon coeur avec les dents
pour qu'ils ne me l'arrachent pas
et le sang qui me couvre
est le sang de mes cris

et ils emportent mon sang
les soldats
qui portent un nuage rempli de morts.

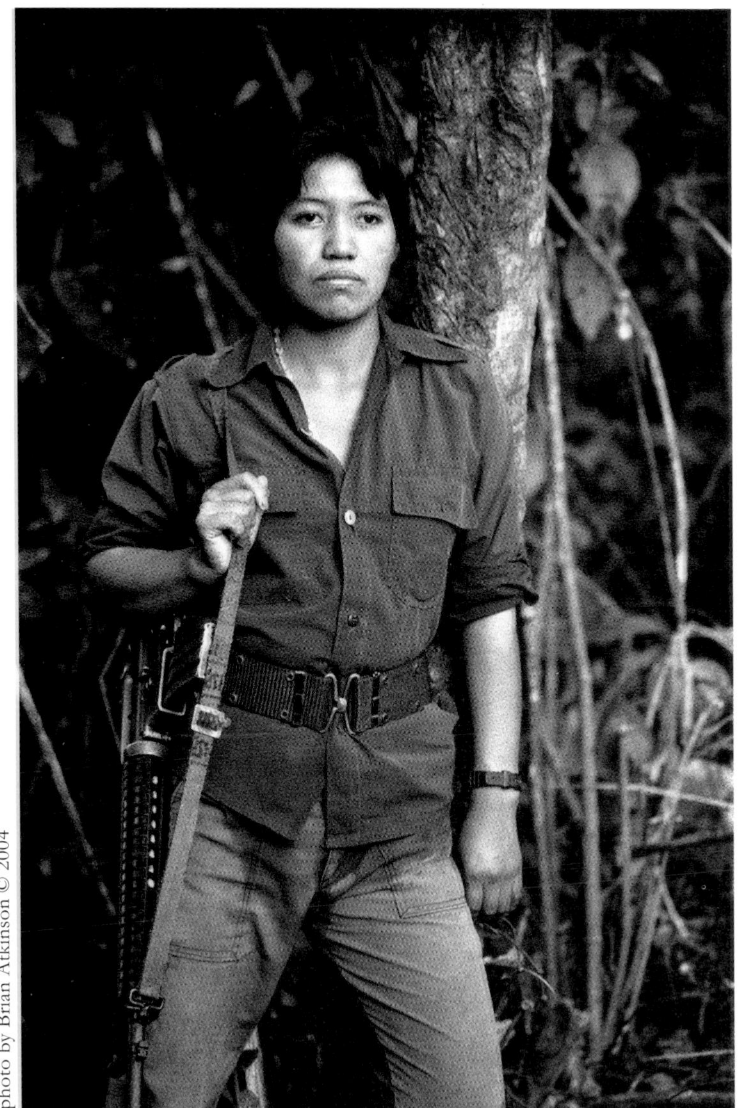

photo by Brian Atkinson © 2004

VI

To María, "la india," with respect

From the hilltop
I saw my people massacred
and rising from the dust
from the teeth from the severed members
I saw the blood in rebellion
like a giant pillar of fire
supporting a heaven of smoke.

From the hilltop
I saw my people devastated
and their tears of fury
turning to dry torrents
of sorrow and suffering.

And I came down
I came slowly down the hill
until I merged
with the severed screams
the open mouths
the swollen stomachs
the curled hands
the rotting cadavers
and I found my people alive!

VI

A María, "la india", con respeto

Desde lo alto del monte
vi mi pueblo masacrado
y levantándose del polvo
de los dientes de los miembros cercenados
vi la sangre en rebelión
como un gigante pilar de fuego
sosteniendo un cielo hecho de humo.

Desde lo alto del monte
vi mi pueblo devastado
y las lágrimas rabiosas
formaban torrentes secos
de dolor y de miseria.

Y bajé
bajé del monte a paso lento
hasta confundirme
con los gritos cercenados
las bocas abiertas
los estómagos hinchados
las manos crispadas
los cadáveres putrefactos
y encontré a mi pueblo vivo!

VI

Pour Maria, «l'Indienne», avec respect

Du haut de la montagne
je vis mon peuple massacré
et se levant de la poussière,
des dents et des membres tronqués
je vis le sang en révolte
comme une gigantesque colonne de feu
soutenant un ciel fait de fumée.

Du haut de la montagne
je vis mon peuple dévasté
et les larmes furieuses
formaient des torrents secs
de douleur et de misère.

Et je descendis
je descendis de la montagne à pas si lents
que je me confondis
avec les cris supprimés
les bouches ouvertes
les ventres tuméfiés
les mains crispées
les cadavres putréfiés
et je trouvai mon peuple vivant!

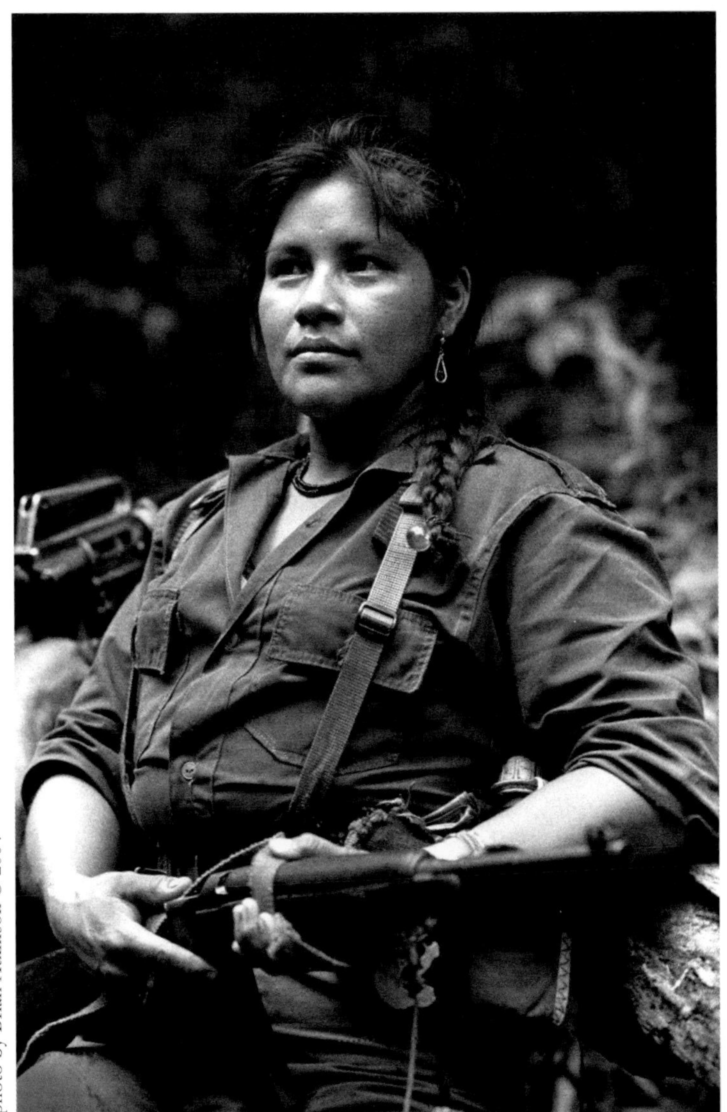

photo by Brian Atkinson © 2004

XXII

To María, "la india", with respect

The ribbon of bullets
for this weapon I hold in my hands
crosses my chest

and with my woman's boot
I grind hard
this ground damp
with the blood of my people

the wind blows my long hair
and I cinch it
with the band of my decision
to fight, to combat
the unjust power and the hunger.

And these starless nights are long
waiting spying calculating not sleeping
always hoping exploring imagining avoiding
the fatal ambush.

thinking thinking becoming tired enjoying the time
I say to myself
        and the future
        is the future of my people
        and I sense it to be mine also
and I smile tentatively
in fear in the ambush happy in the victory
quietly hopefully prepared

but now the hour has come
the revolution is won
and happiness falls to shreds
when they replace my honest rifle
with a cup of coffee
I have to serve to the new executives.

XXII

A María, "la india", con respeto

Cruza mi pecho
la banda de cartuchos
de esta arma que tengo entre las manos

y piso fuerte
con mi bota de mujer
este suelo húmedo
con la sangre de mi pueblo

el viento sacude mi melena
y lo ato fuerte
con el lazo de mi decisión
de luchar, de combatir
el poder injusto y el hambre.

Y son largas estas noches sin estrellas
esperando espiando calculando no durmiendo
siempre esperando tanteando imaginando esquivando
la emboscada fatal

pensando pensando fatigando gozando el tiempo
me digo
          y el futuro
          es el futuro de mi pueblo
          y siento que es el mío también
y sonrío a tientas
con temor por la emboscada con alegría por el triunfo
quietamente esperanzada preparada

pero hoy ha llegado la hora
en que la revolución ha triunfado
y la alegría se cae a pedazos
cuando a mi fusil honesto lo cambian
por la taza de café
que debo servir a los ejecutivos.

XXII

Pour María, «l'Indienne,» avec respect

La bande de cartouches
de cette arme que je tiens entre les mains
croise mon coeur

avec ma botte de femme
je foule d'un pied fort
cette terre humide
du sang de mon peuple

le vent secoue ma chevelure
et je l'attache fort
avec le bandeau de ma décision
de lutter, de combattre
le pouvoir injuste et la faim.

Et elles sont longues ces nuits sans étoiles
passées à attendre à épier à calculer à ne pas dormir
à espérer à tâter à imaginer à éviter toujours
l'embuscade fatale

je me dis
en réfléchissant réfléchissant jouissant du temps
        et le futur
        est le futur de mon peuple
        et je sens que c'est le mien aussi
et je souris toute hésitante
de peur de l'embuscade de joie pour le triomphe
tranquillement préparée pleine d'espoir

mais aujourd'hui est arrivée l'heure
où la révolution a triomphé
et la joie s'émiette
quand ils échangent mon fusil honnête
contre la tasse de café
que je dois servir aux nouveaux exécutifs

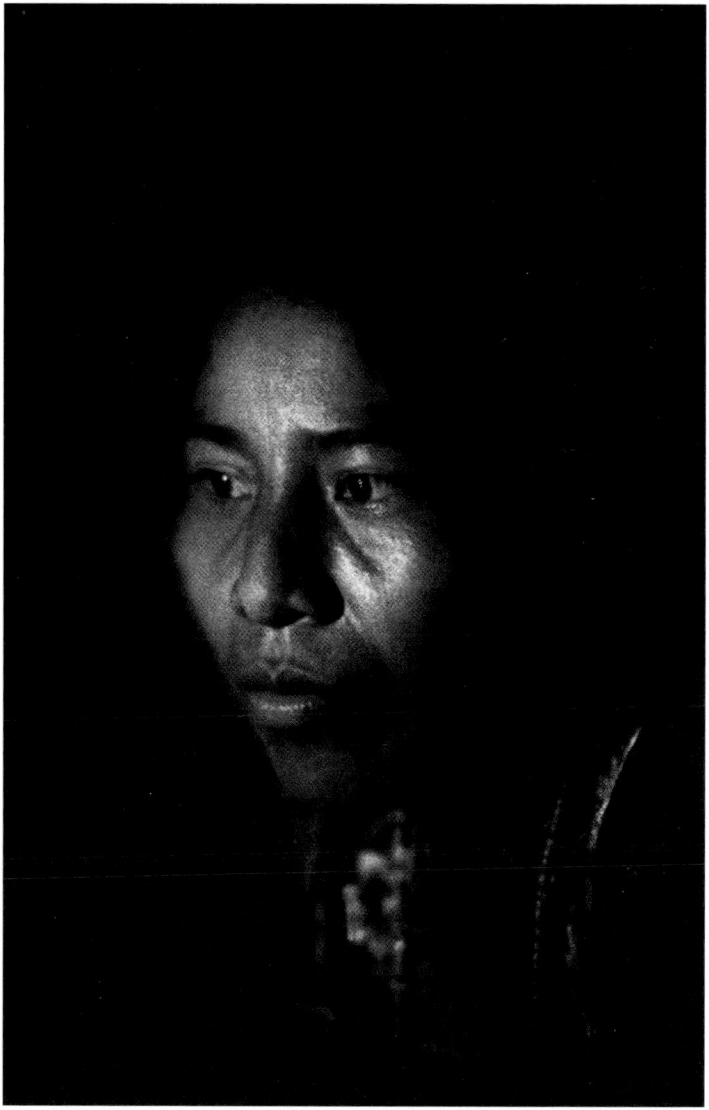

photo by Brian Atkinson © 2004

XXIII

To María José, with respect

and I cry out
I cry out in the streets
of this country that today begins to exist,
that I too fought with my hands my books my ideas

I open the office doors in the white or burned buildings, desk drawers,
filing cabinets, computers, statistics, numbers, wastebins
and I cry out
that I too fought from the classroom the kitchen the office the street

I enter the first aid stations, the private clinics,
hospitals, mausoleums, laboratories, morgues, common graves
and I cry out
that I also got sick suffered died cried over the smell of the dead

I beat on the walls of the unions, the universities, the schools,
the institutions, the ministries, the special commissions,
and I cry out
that I too suffered being trapped persecuted jailed

I appeal to the press, radio, television, news reports, the decrees,
to the critical studies, the conversations, the cafes, the kiosks
the newspaper vendors, the streets
and I cry out

and I cry out
that I also suffered torture
with the same courage, the same certainty, the same conviction,
the same pride, the same valor as the heroic *compañero.*

And I cry out that the freedom of my people
ought to be my freedom too

But tell me tell me
Why should I cry out?

No one will listen to this woman
because the men are celebrating the victory.

XXIII

A María José, con respeto.

y grito
grito en las calles
de este país que hoy empieza a existir
que yo también combatí con mis manos mis libros mis ideas

abro las puertas de los edificios blancos o quemados, de las oficinas,
escritorios, cajones, ficheros, computadoras, estadísticas, números,
basureros
y grito
que yo también luché desde la clase la cocina la oficina la calle

entro en la sala de primeros auxilios, en las clínicas privadas en los
hospitales, en los pabellones, en los laboratorios, en las morgues, en las
fosas comunes
y grito
que yo también me enfermé sufrí morí lloré con el olor de los muertos

golpeo las paredes en los gremios, en las universidades, en las escuelas,
en las instituciones, en los ministerios, en las comisiones especializadas
y grito
que yo también sufrí la persecución el encarcelamiento la encajonada

interpelo la prensa, la radio, la televisión, los informes, los decretos,
los estudios críticos, las conversaciones, los cafés, los kioskos,
los vendedores de diarios, las calles
y grito

y grito
que yo también padecí la tortura
con el mismo coraje, la misma certeza, la misma convicción, la misma arrogancia, el mismo valor del compañero heróico.

Y grito que la libertad de mi pueblo
debe ser también mi libertad.

Pero dime dime
¿por qué debo yo gritar?

Nadie escucha a esta mujer
porque los hombres están festejando la victoria.

XXIII

Pour Maria José, avec respect

et je crie
je crie dans les rues
de ce pays qui aujourd'hui commence à exister
que moi aussi je combattai avec mes mains mes livres mes idées

j'ouvre les portes des édifices blancs ou brûlés, des bureaux,
des tiroirs, des fichiers, des ordinateurs, des statistiques, des numéros, des poubelles
et je crie
que moi aussi je luttai sans cesse dans la salle de classe dans la cuisine dans le bureau dans la rue

j'entre dans les salles d'urgence, dans les cliniques privées, dans les hôpitaux, dans les pavillons, dans les laboratoires, dans les morgues, dans les fosses communes
et je crie
que moi aussi je tombai malade souffrai mourus pleurai à cause de l'odeur des morts

je frappe les murs dans les corporations dans les universités, dans les écoles,
dans les institutions, dans les ministères, dans les commissions spécialisées,
et je crie
que moi aussi je souffrai la persécution l'emprisonnement le supplice

j'interpelle la presse, la radio, la télévision, les rapports, les décrets
les études critiques, les conversations, les cafés, les kiosques
les vendeurs de journaux, les rues
et je crie

et je crie
que moi aussi je souffrai la torture
avec le même courage, la même certitude, la même conviction, la même arrogance, la même fortitude que le *compañero* héroïque.

Et je crie que la liberté de mon peuple
doit être la mienne aussi

Mais dis-moi dis-moi
pourquoi dois-je crier?

Personne n'écoute cette femme
parce que les hommes sont en train de fêter la victoire.

These are poems for peace.
Things happened, do happen that should not happen ever again!

Estos poemas son para la paz.
Hay cosas que pasaron, pasan ¡que no deben pasar nunca más!

Ces poèmes sont pour la paix.
Il y a des choses qui se sont passées, qui se passent, qui ne devraient jamais plus se passer!

About the photographer / Sobre el fotógrafo / Sur le photographe

Brian Atkinson has worked as a professional photographer for the past 17 years. In that time he has traveled to over 50 countries, but the nation that has captured his heart and imagination is Guatemala and the struggles of its Mayan people. Brian is a frequent contributor to *Canadian Geographic*, *Equinox* and *The Globe and Mail*. For Brian, photography is about people, the chance to live, learn and work with people all over the world, and to help them voice their story. To date, Brian has had two books published: *Fredericton* (Halifax NS: Nimbus, 2001) and *Fantastic New Brunswick* (Halifax NS: Nimbus, 2003).

Brian Atkinson ha trabajado como fotógrafo profesional desde hace 17 años. Durante estos años ha viajado a más de 50 países, sin embargo es Guatemala, y la lucha del pueblo maya, lo que ha cautivado su corazón y su imaginación. Brian contribuye frecuentemente en publicaciones como *Canadian Geographic*, *Equinox* y en el periódico *The Globe and Mail*. Para Brian, la fotografía se centra en la gente, en la posibilidad de vivir, aprender y trabajar con gente de todo el mundo, y ayudarles a dar voz a su historia". Hasta la fecha, Brian tiene publicados dos libros: *Fredericton* (Halifax NS: Nimbus, 2001) y *Fantastic New Brunswick* (Halifax NS: Nimbus, 2003).

Brian Atkinson travaille comme photographe professionnel depuis 17 ans. Au cours de ces années, il a voyagé dans plus de 50 pays, mais c'est le Guatemala et la lutte du peuple maya qui ont captivé son coeur et son imagination. Brian contribue fréquemment aux périodiques *Canadian Geographic* et *Equinox* ainsi qu'au journal *The Globe and Mail*. La photographie, qui, selon Brian, est centrée sur les gens, lui permet de vivre, d'apprendre et de travailler chez les gens aux quatre coins du monde, tout en les aidant à exprimer leur histoire. Jusqu'à date, Brian a fait paraître deux livres: *Fredericton* (Halifax N-E: Nimbus, 2001) et *Fantastic New Brunswick* (Halifax N-E: Nimbus, 2003).

About the poet / Sobre la poeta / Sur la poète

Nela Rio (Argentine-Canadian). A poet, writer, artist, and literary critic. Two books of poems published in Spain: *En las noches que desvisten otras noches* (Madrid: Orígenes, 1989); *Aquella luz, la que estremece* (Madrid: Ediciones Torremozas, 1992); and four books, bilingual editions, in Canada: *Túnel de proa verde / Tunnel of the Green Prow*, Hugh Hazelton, translator (Fredericton NB: Broken Jaw Press, 1998, 2004); *Los espejos hacen preguntas / The Mirrors Ask Questions* Elizabeth Gamble Miller, translator (Fredericton NB: Gold Leaf Press, 1999); *Cuerpo amado / Beloved Body,* Hugh Hazelton, translator (Fredericton NB: Broken Jaw Press, 2002); *En las noches que desvisten otras noches / During Nights That Undress Other Nights,* Elizabeth Gamble Miller, translator (Fredericton NB: Broken Jaw Press, 2003). *El espacio de la luz / The Space of Light* a selection of poetry and prose, Elizabeth Gamble Miller, translator, is forthcoming in 2004 from Broken Jaw Press.

Nela Rio (Argentino/canadiense). Poeta, escritora, artista e investigadora. Dos poemarios publicados en España, *En las noches que desvisten otras noches* (Orígenes, Madrid, 1989) y *Aquella luz, la que estremece* (Ediciones Torremozas, Madrid, 1989); cuatro poemarios, ediciones bilingües, en Canadá: *Túnel de proa verde / Tunnel of the Green Prow,* Hugh Hazelton, traductor, (Broken Jaw Press, Fredericton NB, 1998, 2004); *Los espejos hacen preguntas / The Mirrors Ask Questions*, Elizabeth Gamble Miller, traductora, (Gold Leaf Press, Fredericton NB, 1999); *Cuerpo amado / Beloved Body*, Hugh Hazelton, traductor, (Broken Jaw Press, Fredericton NB, 2002); *During Nights That Undress Other Nights / En las noches que desvisten otras noches*, Elizabeth Gamble Miller, traductora, (Broken Jaw Press, Fredericton NB, 2003); de próxima publicación po Broken Jaw Press, en 2004, *El espacio de la luz / The Space of Light,* selección de poemas y cuentos, traducidos por Elizabeth Gamble Miller.

Nela Rio. (Argentine / canadienne). Poète, écrivaine, artiste et critique littéraire. Deux recueils de poèmes publiés en Espagne: *En las noches que desvisten otras noches* (Madrid, Origenes, 1989); *Aquella luz, la que estremece* (Madrid, Ediciones Torremozas, 1992); et quatre livres, des éditions bilingues, au Canada: *Tunel de proa verde / Tunnel of the Green Prow,* traduit par Hugh Hazelton (Fredericton NB: Broken Jaw Press, 1998, 2004); *Los espejos hacen preguntas / The Mirrors Ask Questions,* traduit par Elizabeth Gamble Miller (Fredericton NB : Gold Leaf Press, 1999); *Cuerpo amado / Beloved Body,* traduit par Hugh Hazelton (Fredericton NB: Broken Jaw Press, 2002); *En las noches que desvisten otras noches / During Nights that Undress Other Nights*, traduit par Elizabeth Gamble Miller (Fredericton NB: Broken Jaw Press, 2003). A paraître chez Broken Jaw Press (2004) : *El espacio de la luz / The Space of Light,* recueil de poésie et de prose, traduit par Elizabeth Gamble Miller.

About the translator into English / Sobre la traductora al inglés / Sur la traductrice à l'anglais

Elizabeth Gamble Miller, Ph.D., professor emeritus, Southern Methodist University, translates Spanish poetry, fiction, fable, and essay. Her publications include 15 bilingual editions of authors from Spain, Mexico, Central, and South America. Miller is on the board of *Translation Review*, editor of the newletter of the American Literary Translators Association, and is a corresponding member of the Academia Salvadoreña de la Lengua.

La doctora Elizabeth Gamble Miller, profesora emérita de Southern Methodist University, Dallas, Texas, es traductora del español al inglés de poesía, ensayo y cuento contemporáneo. Entre sus publicaciones tiene 15 ediciones bilingües; ha traducido autores de España, de México, de Centro y Sud América. Miller es miembro del Consejo Editorial de *Translation Review*, y editora del boletín de noticias de la Asociación Americana de Traductores Literarios (ALTA); y es miembro correspondiente de la Academia Salvadoreña de la Lengua.

Elizabeth Gamble Miller, docteure ès lettres et professeure émérite à l'Université Méthodiste du Sud, est traductrice de poésie, de fiction, de fables et d'essais espagnols. Parmi ses publications figurent 15 éditions bilingues; elle a traduit des auteur/e/s de l'Espagne, du Mexique, de l'Amérique centrale et de l'Amérique du sud. Elle siège au conseil de direction du périodique *Translation Review*; elle est rédactrice du bulletin d'information de l'Association américaine de traducteurs littéraires (ALTA), et elle est membre de l'Academia Salvadoreña de la Lengua.

About the translator into French / Sobre la traductora al francés / Sur la traductrice au français

Jill Valéry is a writer and literary translator. She has written extensively on French Canadian literature, and translates from English and Spanish. Her publications include the essay on Francophone Canada in *Longman Anthology of World Literature by Women* (New York: Longman, 1989). Her most recent work, a translation of poems written by Fred Cogswell, appeared in *ellipse* magazine. Jill Valéry lives in Fredericton, New Brunswick.

Jill Valéry es escritora y traductora literaria. Ha escrito numerosos artículos sobre literatura franco-canadiense; tiene traducciones del inglés y del español. Sus publicaciones incluyen el ensayo sobre el Canadá francófono en la *Longman Anthology of World Literature by Women* (New York : Longman, 1989). Su obra más reciente, la traducción de poemas de Fred Cogswell, ha sido publicada en la revista *ellipse*. Jill Valéry vive en Fredericton, New Brunswick.

Jill Valéry est écrivaine et traductrice littéraire. Elle a rédigé de nombreux articles sur la littérature canadienne-française; elle traduit de l'anglais et de l'espagnol. Ses publications comprennent l'essai sur le Canada francophone dans *Longman Anthology of World Literature by Women* (New York : Longman, 1989). Son oeuvre la plus récente est une traduction de poèmes de Fred Cogswell, qui a paru dans la revue *ellipse*. Jill Valéry vit à Fredericton, dans le Nouveau Brunswick.

About the editor / Sobre el editor / Sur le rédacteur

Joe Blades is publisher of Broken Jaw Press Inc.; a visual artist; the community radio producer/host of *Ashes, Paper & Beans: Fredericton's Writing & Art Show* (CHSR). His poetry books are *Cover Makes a Set* (London ON: SpareTime Editions, 1990), *River Suite* (Toronto: Insomniac Press, 1998), *Open Road West* (Fredericton NB: Broken Jaw Press, 2000, 2001), and *Casemate Poems* (Waterloo ON: Widows and Orphans, 2004).

Joe Blades es el editor de Broken Jaw Press Inc; poeta, artista, y productor/director del programa radial *Ashes, Paper & Beans: Fredericton's Writing & Art Show* (CHSR). Entre sus poemarios, *Cover Makes a Set* (London ON: SpareTime Editions, 1990), *River Suite* (Toronto: Insomniac Press, 1998), *Open Road West* (Fredericton NB: Broken Jaw Press, 2000, 2001) y and *Casemate Poems* (Waterloo ON: Widows and Orphans, 2004).

Joe Blades est l'éditeur de Broken Jaw Press Inc.; poète, artiste et réalisateur/animateur de l'émission de radio *Ashes, Paper & Beans : Fredericton's Writing & Art Show* (CHSR). Ses recueils de poèmes comprennent *Cover Makes a Set* (London, ON : SpareTime Editions, 1990), *River Suite* (Toronto : Insomniac Press, 1998), *Open Road West* (Fredericton NB : Broken Jaw Press, 2000, 2001) et *Casemate Poems* (Waterloo ON: Widows and Orphans, 2004).

Selected Titles in Print

Mulilingual books and translations into English

Cuerpo amado / Beloved Body (Nela Rio; Hugh Hazelton, translator) poetry, 1-896647-81-2

Dark Seasons (Georg Trakl; Robin Skelton, translator) poetry, 0-921411-22-7

During Nights That Undress Other Nights/ En las noches que desvisten otras noches (Nela Rio; Elizabeth Gamble Miller, translator) poetry, 1-55391-008-7

Heaven of Small Moments (Allan Cooper) original poetry, plus translations of Lin Chu, Lorca, Mirabai, Rumi, *et al*, 0-921411-79-0

Herbarium of Souls (Vladimir Tasic; Ralph Bogert, Christine Pribichevich-Zoric & Vladimir Tasic, translators) short fiction, 0-921411-72-3

I Love You: 65 international poets poets united against violence against women (Gino d'Artali, ed.) poetry in English or Spanish, 0-921411-31-6

Sunset (Pablo Urbanyi; Hugh Hazelton, translator) novel, 1-55391-014-1

Túnel de proa verde / Tunnel of the Green Prow (Nela Rio; Hugh Hazelton, translator) poetry, second edition, 1-896647-10-3

Some of our other titles

All the Perfect Disguises (Lorri Neilsen Glenn) poetry, 1-55391-010-9

Antimatter (Hugh Hazelton) poetry, 1-896647-98-7

Avoidance Tactics (Sky Gilbert) drama, 1-896647-50-2

Bathory (Moynan King) drama, 1-896647-36-7

Break the Silence (Denise DeMoura) poetry, 1-896647-87-1

Day of the Dog-tooth Violets (Christina Kilbourne) fiction, 1-896647-44-8

Mangoes on the Maple Tree (Uma Parameswaran) fiction, 1-896647-79-0

Manitoba highway map (rob mclennan) poetry, 0-921411-89-8

Paper Hotel (rob mclennan) poetry, 1-55391-004-4

resume drowning (Jon Paul Fiorentino) poetry, 1-896647-94-4

Shadowy:Technicians: New Ottawa Poets (rob mclennan, editor), poetry, 0-921411-71-5

Song of the Vulgar Starling (Eric Miller) poetry, 0-921411-93-6

Starting from Promise (Lorne Dufour) poetry, 1-896647-52-9

Tales for an Urban Sky (Alice Major) poetry, 1-896647-11-1

The Longest Winter (Julie Doiron, Ian Roy) photos, short fiction, 0-921411-95-2

The Robbie Burns Revival & Other Stories (Cecilia Kennedy) short fiction, 1-55391-024-9

This Day Full of Promise (Michael Dennis) poetry, 1-896647-48-0

The Yoko Ono Project (Jean Yoon) drama, 1-55391-001-X

What Was Always Hers (Uma Parameswaran) short fiction, 1-896647-12-X

www.brokenjaw.com hosts our current catalogue, book prices, submissions guidelines, manuscript award competitions, booktrade sales representation and distribution information. Directly from us, all individual orders must be prepaid. All Canadian orders must add 7% GST/HST (CCRA Business Number 892667403RT0001).

Broken Jaw Press Inc., Box 596 Stn A, Fredericton NB E3B 5A6, Canada